THE 47 BEST
CHOCOLATE CHIP COOKIES
IN THE WORLD

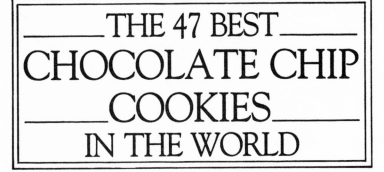

THE 47 BEST
CHOCOLATE CHIP
COOKIES
IN THE WORLD

The Recipes That Won the
National Chocolate Chip Cookie Contest

LARRY AND HONEY ZISMAN

St. Martin's Press
New York

Design by Laura Hammond

13

Library of Congress Cataloging in Publication Data

Zisman, Larry.
  The 47 best chocolate chip cookies in the world.

  1. Cookies.   I. Zisman, Honey.   II. Title.
III. Title: Forty-seven best chocolate chip cookies in
the world.   IV. Title: Chocolate chip cookies in the
world.
TX772.Z57   1983   641.8'654   83-9658
ISBN 0-312-29983-4 (pbk.)

*For all those millions and millions of people
who have made the chocolate chip cookie
the undisputed number one favorite*

CONTENTS

Our sincere thanks to all the cookie bakers who sent us their most delicious chocolate chip cookie recipes and who made this contest so difficult—but a real joy—to judge.

A thank you also to all the journalists who spread the news about the contest and helped to make it such a success.

And, finally, a special thank you to our friends and associates who baked and ate more chocolate chip cookies than they ever thought existed.

THE CREATION OF THE FIRST
CHOCOLATE CHIP COOKIE

1930 was not the happiest year in American history. The stock market had come crashing down the year before and the Great Depression was just beginning.

But, in a small shoe-manufacturing town in Massachusetts about twenty miles south of Boston, something very good was about to happen.

Until 1930, the most notable thing about Whitman, Massachusetts, was that a young man named Paul Revere had spent some time in a local foundry learning how to make cannons. In 1930, however, something else was to happen that would affect just about every person in the country.

In that year Ruth and Kenneth Wakefield opened a new restaurant in a historic house in Whitman that local legend said was once the home of Frank Vinny Smith, the noted American marine painter. Since the house was across the road from the toll gates on the old Boston-to-New Bedford Turnpike, the Wakefields named their new restaurant the Toll House.

The couple was exceptionally well qualified to own and operate a restaurant. Ruth had a degree in dietetics from Framingham State College, and Kenneth had been a steward for a steamship line. For thirty-seven years, until 1967 when they sold the restaurant and retired, the

Wakefields were well-known and gracious hosts, offering outstanding food and elegant service in a colonial atmosphere. *Life* magazine featured the Toll House as one of the finest places to dine in the United States.

But all that success came after 1930, when the Wakefields, like millions of others, were learning to make do with less during the hardest economic times in American history.

One day Ruth Wakefield was preparing a batch of Butter Drop-Do cookies, a favorite recipe dating from colonial times, that called for nuts. But since she had none, she cut up a semisweet chocolate bar and added the small bits and pieces of chocolate to the cookie dough. Mrs. Wakefield expected the pieces of chocolate to melt; but instead of melting, the pieces of chocolate remained hard—and, quite unexpectedly, the chocolate chip cookie was created.

The fantastic new chocolate chip cookie was an instant success, and both the cookie and the Toll House became famous throughout the whole country.

During World War II, the Wakefields sent chocolate chip cookies to American servicemen all over the world.

After seeing the great popularity of her cookie creation, Mrs. Wakefield got in touch with the Nestlé Company, the manufacturer of the chocolate bar she had cut up to use in place of the nuts for her Drop-Do recipe. At her suggestion, the company began making a chocolate bar that was scored so it could be broken up into small pieces for everyone who wanted to make their own chocolate chip cookies. A special chopper was also included to help break the chocolate up into little pieces.*

The next step was the introduction of small pieces of chocolate—the chocolate chips that are so well loved today.

The chocolate chip cookie created by Ruth Wakefield is now known everywhere, of course, as the Toll House cookie.

The present owners of the Toll House restaurant, David and Donald Saccone, have a small factory in the back where they make about 15,000 pounds of chocolate chip cookies each week. The cookies are now sold in retail shops in New England, but the Saccones hope to expand throughout the United States so that the original Toll House cookies can be enjoyed from coast to coast—just as the many variations on this delicious theme already are.

---

* According to Nestlé, the company that made the chocolate bar that Ruth Wakefield cut up in 1930 to create the first chocolate chip cookie, home bakers in the United States during 1982 made more than 7 billion chocolate chip cookies using Toll House Morsels from Nestlé.

ORIGINAL TOLL HOUSE® COOKIES

© by the Nestlé Company

2¼ cups sifted flour
1 teaspoon baking soda
1 teaspoon salt
1 cup softened butter or shortening
¾ cup granulated sugar
¾ cup brown sugar, firmly packed
1 teaspoon vanilla
½ teaspoon water
2 eggs
1 12-ounce package (2 cups) Semi-Sweet Real
    Chocolate Morsels
1 cup coarsely chopped nuts

Preheat oven to 375° F.

Sift together flour, baking soda, and salt; set aside. Combine butter or shortening, sugar, brown sugar, vanilla, and water; beat till creamy. Beat in eggs. Add flour mixture; mix well. Stir in Semi-Sweet Real Chocolate Morsels and nuts. Drop by well-rounded half teaspoonfuls onto greased cookie sheets. Bake for 10 to 12 minutes. Makes 100 two-inch cookies.

FAMOUS AMOS RAISIN-FILLED CHOCOLATE CHIP COOKIES

1 cup (2 sticks) margarine, softened
¾ cup light brown sugar, firmly packed
¾ cup granulated sugar
1 teaspoon vanilla
1 teaspoon water
2 medium-sized eggs
2½ cups sifted all-purpose flour
1 teaspoon baking soda
½ teaspoon salt
2 cups raisins
1 package (12 ounces) semisweet chocolate pieces

Preheat oven to 375° F.

Beat softened margarine, brown and white sugars, vanilla, water, and eggs in a large bowl with electric mixer until creamy and thoroughly blended. By hand, stir in flour, baking soda, and salt until well mixed. Stir in raisins and chocolate pieces. Using teaspoon from measuring set, spoon dough by teaspoonfuls onto cookie sheets. Allow 1 to 1½ inches between cookies for spreading. Bake for 8 minutes, or until cookies are nicely browned, depending on how crisp or well done you like them. Makes about 6 dozen.

REESE'S COOKIES

*1 cup shortening or ¾ cup butter or margarine,
   softened*
1 cup granulated sugar
½ cup brown sugar, firmly packed
1 teaspoon vanilla
2 eggs
2 cups unsifted all-purpose flour
1 teaspoon baking soda
1 cup Reese's Peanut Butter Flavored Chips
1 cup Hershey's Semi-Sweet Chocolate Chips

Preheat oven to 350° F.

Cream shortening *or* butter or margarine, sugar, brown sugar, and vanilla until light and fluffy. Add eggs and beat well. Combine flour and baking soda; add to creamed mixture. Stir in peanut butter chips and chocolate chips. Drop by teaspoonfuls onto ungreased cookie sheet. Bake for 10 to 12 minutes or until lightly browned. Cool slightly; remove to wire rack and cool completely. Makes about 5 dozen 2½-inch cookies.

THE FAMOUS CHOCOLATE CHIP COOKIE

      ¾ lb. butter
      ½ cup granulated sugar
      1 cup brown sugar
      ¼ teaspoon vanilla
      ¼ teaspoon salt
      4 eggs
      3½ cups flour
      ¼ teaspoon baking soda
      1 package (6 ounces) semisweet chocolate chips

Preheat oven to 350° F.

Mix butter, white and brown sugar at slow speed for 2 minutes; add vanilla, salt, and eggs. Mix ingredients for 1 minute at slow speed, then for 2 minutes at high speed. Add flour and baking soda; mix until flour is blended into a smooth dough. Add chocolate chips and mix for 1 minute at low speed. Spoon off cookies onto cookie pan and bake for approximately 8 minutes.

YULETIDE CHOCOLATE CHIP COOKIES

From the Ghirardelli Original Chocolate Cookbook, Second Edition, copyrighted 1982 by the Ghirardelli Chocolate Company; reprinted with permission of the Ghirardelli Chocolate Company. Ghirardelli is a registered trademark of the Golden Grain Macaroni Company.

½ cup butter or margarine, softened
⅔ cup packed brown sugar, firmly packed
1 teaspoon brandy flavoring
3 tablespoons dark corn syrup
1 egg
1 cup diced candied mixed fruit
1⅓ cups flour
1 teaspoon pumpkin pie spice
¾ teaspoon baking powder
¼ teaspoon salt
1 package (6 ounces) Ghirardelli Semi-Sweet
   Chocolate Chips
⅓ cup chopped pecans
⅓ cup slivered almonds
⅓ cup currants
14 red candied cherries, quartered

Preheat oven to 350° F.

Cream butter with brown sugar, brandy flavoring, and corn syrup; add egg and beat until very light. Coat candied fruit with 1 tablespoon of the flour; set aside. Sift remaining flour with pumpkin pie spice, baking powder, and salt. Stir dry ingredients into creamed mixture. Add fruit, chocolate chips, pecans, almonds, and currants. Chill dough 1 hour. Drop by heaping teaspoon onto greased baking sheet. Top each cookie with piece of cherry. Bake for 8 to 10 minutes. Cool on rack. Store in covered containers several days to soften and age. Makes 4½ dozen cookies.

THE NATIONAL CHOCOLATE CHIP COOKIE CONTEST

There are more different kinds of contests than any one person can count but what could be more worthwhile and rewarding than a search for the best chocolate chip cookies in the world?

Looking forward to collecting, cataloging, baking, eating, and choosing the best chocolate chip cookies, we sent contest announcements to hundreds of newspapers and magazines, describing the competition and offering honor and recognition for the elite of this great American classic.

The news went out and the cookies came back. We received over 3,000 recipes, from the rocky coast of Maine to the flowered islands of Hawaii, from the mist of Puget Sound in Washington State to the Everglades in Florida.

We received recipes for big cookies and little cookies, for hard cookies and soft cookies, and for round cookies and square cookies. There were cookies with nuts and cookies with fruit, cookies with oatmeal and cookies with rum, cookies with yogurt and cookies with wheat germ. But all the cookies had one ingredient in common: chocolate chips.

Recipes were sorted, recorded, and studied, and cookies were mixed, baked, and eaten. And finally, after baking and eating more cookies than all of us together had ever seen, the best chocolate chip cookies in the world were chosen.

There were cheers for the winners but no tears for the others, because every cookie with chocolate chips is, by any measure, a winner, too.

THE RECIPES FOR THE 47 BEST CHOCOLATE CHIP COOKIES IN THE WORLD

PEANUT CLUSTER SUPREME

Rosemary Kay   Tacoma, Washington

1 cup granulated sugar
2 eggs
3 teaspoons vanilla
4 teaspoons unsifted all-purpose flour
2 jars (12 ounces each) dry-roasted peanuts
1 package (12 ounces) chocolate chips

Preheat oven to 350° F.

Combine the sugar, eggs, vanilla, and flour in blender and mix on high for 2 minutes. Remove to bowl; stir in peanuts and chocolate chips. Drop dough by tablespoonfuls onto greased cookie sheets, 3 inches apart, and bake for 10 to 12 minutes. Remove immediately from baking sheets and cool on racks. Makes 4 dozen large cookies.

Note: This recipe works in a food processor, too.

Cookie dough can also be spread in a 13 × 9½ × 2-inch baking dish and baked for 18 to 20 minutes, or until it springs back when tested. Let cool and then cut into squares. Makes about 30 two-inch square cookies.

MOCHA CHIP BARS

Pat Sullivan   Rochester, New York

2½ cups sifted all-purpose flour
½ teaspoon baking powder
¼ teaspoon salt
1 cup butter
1 cup brown sugar, firmly packed
1 teaspoon vanilla
1½ tablespoons instant coffee powder
1 package (6 ounces) chocolate chips
½ cup chopped nuts

Preheat oven to 350° F.

Sift together flour, baking powder, and salt; set aside. Beat together butter, sugar, vanilla, and instant coffee powder. Add dry ingredients. Mix well. Stir in chocolate chips and chopped nuts. Press dough into greased 15 × 10 × 1-inch baking pan. Bake for 20 to 25 minutes, or until lightly browned. Cut into bars of desired size while still warm. Makes about 30 large cookies or 60 small cookies.

The biggest chocolate sculpture ever made was a 4,484-pound, 10-foot-high Easter egg that was constructed in Melbourne, Australia.

BAVARIAN-MINT CHIPPERS

Cypress Vollmer   Forks, Washington

2½ cups unsifted all-purpose flour
1 teaspoon baking soda
1 teaspoon salt
1 cup butter, softened
¾ cup granulated sugar
¾ cup brown sugar, firmly packed
2 eggs
¾ teaspoon mint extract
2 teaspoons instant coffee powder dissolved in 1
     tablespoon hot water
1 package (12 ounces) chocolate chips
1 cup chopped almonds

Preheat oven to 375° F.

Sift together flour, baking soda, and salt; set aside. Beat butter with both sugars. Add eggs, beating well. Add mint extract and coffee. Add dry ingredients and mix well. Stir in chocolate chips and nuts. Drop by teaspoonfuls onto greased cookie sheets, about 2 inches apart. Bake for 8 to 10 minutes. Cool on racks. Makes about 100 cookies.

CHOCOLATE DROP OATMEAL COOKIES

Margaret Ann Pietrosky   Fort Collins, Colorado

¾ cup unsifted all-purpose flour
½ teaspoon baking soda
½ teaspoon salt
½ cup shortening
½ cup brown sugar
½ cup granulated sugar
1 egg
1 teaspoon vanilla
1½ cups uncooked oatmeal granola
½ cup semisweet chocolate chips

Preheat oven to 350° F.

Sift together flour, baking soda, and salt; set aside. Beat shortening with sugars. Add egg and vanilla and beat well. Add sifted dry ingredients, then oatmeal granola and chocolate chips. Drop by teaspoonfuls onto greased cookie sheets, about 2 inches apart. Bake 10 minutes. Makes 4 dozen cookies.

CHOCO-NUT DAINTIES

Carol Ingemi   Hammonton, New Jersey

1 cup margarine (or more as needed), softened
¾ cup granulated sugar
1 egg
1½ teaspoons vanilla
2 cups unsifted all-purpose flour
1 teaspoon salt
2 packages (one 12-ounce and one 6-ounce)
   semisweet chocolate chips
1 cup chopped nuts

Preheat oven to 350° F.

Mix together, by hand, ¾ cup of the margarine, the sugar, egg, and vanilla until well blended. Combine flour and salt, then blend into egg mixture. Mix in the 6-ounce package chocolate chips. Shape dough by hand into logs 2 inches long. Place on ungreased cookie sheet. Bake for 12 to 14 minutes. Cool on racks.

Meanwhile, melt the 12-ounce package chocolate chips and remaining ¼ cup margarine over hot water. Stir until smooth. If mixture is too thick, add more margarine, 1 tablespoon at a time, until it is the right consistency.

Dip ends of cookies into chocolate coating and roll in nuts. Place on racks or on wax paper until set. Makes about 50 cookies.

BRANDYWINE SANDWICH COOKIES

Gertrude Lilian Tomic   Wilmington, Delaware

COOKIES

1½ cups unsifted all-purpose flour
½ teaspoon baking powder
½ teaspoon baking soda
½ cup butter
2 squares unsweetened chocolate
½ cup brown sugar
½ cup granulated sugar
1 teaspoon vanilla
½ cup sour cream or buttermilk
1 egg
½ cup finely chopped pecans
1 package (6 ounces) semisweet chocolate chips

COFFEE BRANDY FROSTING

½ cup unsalted butter
2 tablespoons unsweetened cocoa powder
1 tablespoon instant coffee powder dissolved in 1
    tablespoon water
2½ cups confectioner's sugar
1½ teaspoons brandy

CHOCOLATE GLAZE

2 ounces (2 squares) semisweet baking chocolate
1 tablespoon brandy or 1 tablespoon coffee
3 tablespoons butter

Preheat oven to 375° F.

Stir together flour, baking powder, and baking soda and set aside. Melt together butter and unsweetened chocolate. Cool. Beat into cooled chocolate mixture the sugars, vanilla, sour cream or buttermilk, and egg. Stir in flour mixture, pecans, and chocolate chips. Roll batter into balls the size of a tablespoon and place 2 inches apart on a greased cookie sheet. Dip the bottom of a drinking glass into granulated sugar and flatten balls of dough. Bake for about 10 minutes; do not overbake. Cool on racks.

Meanwhile, make frosting. Beat together butter and cocoa powder. Add sugar, coffee, and brandy. Beat until fluffy. If cream is too stiff, add a few drops of water at a time to make a better spreading consistency. Sandwich the cookies.

Make glaze by melting chocolate and brandy or coffee in small saucepan over hot water, stirring until smooth. Stir in butter, 1 tablespoon at a time. Drizzle glaze on sandwiched cookie. Let cool and set. Store in airtight container. Makes about 30 double sandwich cookies.

> *The scientific name of chocolate, Theobroma caca, given in 1720 by the Swedish botanist Carolus Linnaeus, comes from the Greek words "cacoa, the food of the gods."*

OATMEAL PEANUT BUTTER WONDERS

Grace Schober   Millbury, Ohio

3 cups sifted all-purpose flour
1 teaspoon baking soda
½ teaspoon baking powder
½ teaspoon salt
1 cup margarine
¾ cup peanut butter
¾ cup brown sugar
¾ cup granulated sugar
2 eggs
1 teaspoon vanilla
1 cup sour cream
2½ cups quick oatmeal
1 package (12 ounces) chocolate chips

Preheat oven to 350° F.

Sift together flour, baking soda, baking powder, and salt; set aside.

Beat together margarine and peanut butter until smooth. Gradually add the sugars, mixing until well blended. Add eggs, one at a time, beating thoroughly after each one. Add vanilla.

Add flour mixture to peanut butter mixture in three additions and sour cream in two, beginning and ending with flour. Mix well after each addition. Add oatmeal and chocolate chips and blend well.

Scoop dough with a small ice cream dipper and place on lightly greased cookie sheet. Grease bottom of drinking glass, dip in sugar, and then press the balls of dough down to a thickness of ⅜ inch. Bake for about 20 minutes (10 minutes on bottom rack and then 10 minutes on upper rack). Cool on racks and store in a tight container. Makes about 3 dozen cookies.

MERINGUE TEASERS

Mrs. John E. Banks   San Antonio, Texas

2 egg whites, lightly beaten
⅔ cup granulated sugar
Pinch of salt
1 teaspoon vanilla
Green food color (optional)
1 cup chocolate chips
1 cup chopped nuts

Preheat oven to 350° F.

Beat egg whites lightly and gradually add sugar. Keep beating until very stiff. Beat in salt, vanilla, and color, if wanted. Fold in chocolate chips and nuts. Cover cookie sheet with aluminum foil and drop cookies by teaspoonfuls onto foil. Place in oven. *Turn oven off and forget.* Do *not* open door for at least 6 hours, or leave overnight. Makes about 50 cookies.

The legendary lover Casanova claimed that chocolate was more effective than champagne for inducing romance.

COCONUT BIGGIES

Jan Thompson   Fairfax, Virginia

1 1/3 cups unsifted hard-wheat flour
1 teaspoon baking soda
1/4 teaspoon salt
4 tablespoons butter
1/4 cup shortening
1/2 cup granulated sugar
1/4 cup dark brown sugar
1 large egg
1 teaspoon vanilla
1/2 cup coarsely chopped walnuts
1/4 cup flaked coconut
1/4 cup chocolate chips

Preheat oven to 375° F.

Mix together flour, baking soda, and salt. Beat together butter, shortening, and sugars. Add egg and vanilla and beat well. Add dry ingredients. Mix in walnuts, coconut, and chocolate chips. Divide dough into 12 equal parts. Flatten each part into a 3½ inch round. Place on greased baking sheet and bake on lowest shelf of oven for 15 minutes. Even if cookies look underbaked, take them out. Cool on racks. Makes 12 large cookies.

APPLESAUCE SPICE COOKIES

Kim Szenzenstein   Oceanport, New Jersey

2 cups sifted all-purpose flour
1 teaspoon baking soda
¼ teaspoon salt
1 teaspoon ground cinnamon
½ teaspoon ground nutmeg
½ cup butter or margarine
½ cup granulated sugar
½ cup dark brown sugar, firmly packed
1 egg
1 cup applesauce
1 cup rolled oats
½ cup seedless raisins
½ cup chopped nuts
½ cup semisweet chocolate chips

Preheat oven to 375° F.

Sift together flour, baking soda, salt, cinnamon, and nutmeg; set aside. In a large bowl, using an electric mixer, beat butter and gradually add the sugars. Beat until light and fluffy. Add egg and beat until blended. On low speed, add applesauce and sifted dry ingredients. Beat just until all ingredients are blended together, using a rubber spatula to scrape down sides of bowl. Stir in the oats, raisins, nuts, and chocolate chips. Drop dough by level tablespoonfuls onto ungreased cookie sheets, about 1 inch apart. Bake 8 minutes, or until cookies are lightly browned. Remove immediately from cookie sheets to racks to cool completely. Makes about 5 dozen.

Two workers in Switzerland were arrested in 1980 for trying to sell state secrets to China and Russia. The information they were offering included forty recipes for making chocolate.

OATMEAL YUMMIES

Dorothy Seamster   Harrison, Arkansas

1½ cups all-purpose flour
3 cups quick oatmeal
½ teaspoon salt
1 teaspoon baking soda
1 cup shortening
1 cup granulated sugar
1 cup brown sugar
2 eggs
1 teaspoon vanilla
2 tablespoons water
1 package (6 ounces) semisweet chocolate chips

Preheat oven to 350° F.

Stir together flour, oatmeal, salt, and baking soda; set aside. Beat together shortening and sugars. Beat in eggs and vanilla until well combined. Add half the dry ingredients; stir well. Add water and other half of the dry ingredients. Stir in chocolate chips. Drop by teaspoonfuls on greased cookie sheets, about 1 inch apart. Bake 7 to 10 minutes. Cool on racks. Makes about 80 cookies.

Of all the chocolate chip enterprises, easily the best known is The Famous Amos Chocolate Chip Cookie. The company was founded by Wally Amos, a former theatrical agent, with financial backing from several Hollywood notables, including Helen Reddy, Bill Cosby, and Marvin Gaye.

Managing his chocolate chip cookie just like he would any other important celebrity, he has fashioned Famous Amos bumper stickers, T-shirts, buttons, gold-plated chocolate chip pendants, cookie jars, baseball caps, and even posters. Personal television appearances by Amos extolling his cookie have included ABC's Good Morning America, the Mike Douglas Show, the Dinah Shore Show, and the Merv Griffin Show.

The Famous Amos Chocolate Chip Cookie is sold not only in the company's own stores but also in some of the most prestigious stores in America: Bloomingdales, Neiman-Marcus, Hudson's, John Wanamaker, and Marshall Field.

Encourage your cookies as they bake . . . talk to them and watch them closely. It might be necessary to turn the tray around if your oven bakes unevenly. Give your cookies love and they'll grow up to be very pretty and tasty. Good luck, and have a very brown day.

—Famous Amos

CHOCOLATE CHIP PISTACHIO COOKIES

Estelle K. Gliffe Palos Hills, Illinois

3 cups unsifted all-purpose flour
1 teaspoon salt
2 teaspoons baking powder
1 cup butter or margarine
1 cup granulated sugar
2 eggs
2 tablespoons milk
1 teaspoon vanilla
¼ cup chopped nuts
1 package pistachio pudding mix
1 package (6 ounces) chocolate chips
Confectioner's sugar (optional)

Preheat oven to 375° F.

Sift together flour, salt, and baking powder; set aside. Beat together butter and sugar. Add eggs, milk, and vanilla and beat until creamy. Add dry ingredients, stirring with hands or spoon until stiff dough forms.

Take out one quarter of the dough and put into a small bowl. Add chopped nuts to this mixture. Add pistachio pudding mix and all but ¼ cup of the chocolate chips to the remaining dough. Shape teaspoonfuls of this dough into balls and place about 1½ inches apart on a lightly greased cookie sheet. Cover bottom of a drinking glass with a damp cloth and flatten balls of dough.

Shape chopped-nut dough mixture into marble-sized balls and place on top of flattened pistachio cookies. Lightly place one of the reserved chocolate chips into each marble-sized ball of dough, pointed side up. Bake for 8 to 10 minutes, or until done. Cool on racks. If desired, dust with confectioners sugar. Makes about 5 dozen cookies.

Chocolate was introduced into Europe in 1528 by the great Spanish explorer Hernando Cortez, who brought it back from Mexico. It became an instant hit with King Charles V and his royal court, and, by using monks hidden away in monasteries to process the cocoa beans, chocolate remained a Spanish secret for nearly one hundred years.

The secret was finally let out by an Italian traveler named Antonio Carletti, who took some chocolate home with him from Spain. It was quickly embraced by the Italian rulers, and, then, through a series of royal marriages, chocolate spread from Italy to Austria, from Austria to France, and from France to England.

ORANGE CREAM CHIPS

Eleanor Hummel   Lavelle, Pennsylvania

2 cups sifted all-purpose flour
1 teaspoon salt
1 cup shortening
1 package (3 ounces) cream cheese, softened
1 cup granulated sugar
2 eggs
2 teaspoons orange juice or orange flavoring
1 package (6 ounces) semisweet chocolate chips

Preheat oven to 350° F.

Sift together flour and salt; set aside. Beat together shortening, cream cheese, and sugar. Beat in eggs, one at a time. Beat in orange juice or orange flavoring; then add dry ingredients. Mix well. Stir in chocolate chips. Drop by teaspoonfuls on greased cookie sheets, 2 inches apart. Bake for 12 minutes. Cool on racks. Makes about 70 cookies.

The United States makes more chocolate than any other country and is followed, in turn, by West Germany, the Netherlands, and Great Britain. Pennsylvania is the leading state in chocolate production.

CHOCOLATE PUDDING AND CREAM DREAMS

Rosie Lichte   Loganville, Wisconsin

2 eggs, beaten
1 cup sour cream
½ cup butter, softened
2 cups packaged biscuit mix
2 packages (4½ ounces each) instant chocolate
    pudding mix
1 package (6 ounces) semisweet chocolate chips
½ cup chopped nuts

Preheat oven to 350° F.
Stir together eggs, sour cream, butter, biscuit mix, and pudding mix. Stir in chocolate chips and nuts. Drop by teaspoonfuls onto ungreased cookie sheets. Bake about 12 minutes. Makes 6 dozen cookies.

HAZELNUT FLAKIES

Gloria B. Williams   Moorestown, New Jersey

1 cup unsifted all-purpose flour
½ teaspoon baking powder
½ teaspoon baking soda
½ teaspoon salt
⅓ cup butter
½ cup granulated sugar
½ cup brown sugar, firmly packed
1 egg
1 teaspoon vanilla
1 cup Grapenuts Flakes
½ cup chopped hazelnuts (filberts)
1 package (6 ounces) chocolate chips

Preheat oven to 375° F.

Mix together flour, baking powder, baking soda, and salt; set aside. Beat butter; blend in sugars and beat well. Beat in egg and vanilla. Add dry ingredients, cereal, nuts, and chocolate chips, mixing until just blended. Drop by teaspoonfuls on ungreased baking sheets, about 2 inches apart. Bake for about 10 minutes; do not overbake. Cookies will puff up and then flatten. Cool slightly in pan before removing to racks to cool. Makes about 2 dozen cookies.

CHIP-ON-CHIP COOKIES

Lucille Boyce   Burbank, California

1 cup plus 2 tablespoons all-purpose flour
½ teaspoon baking soda
¼ teaspoon salt
½ cup butter or shortening
¾ cup light brown sugar, firmly packed
1 teaspoon vanilla
1 egg, well beaten
¾ cup (6 ounces) chocolate chips
¾ cup potato chips, crushed

Preheat oven to 375° F.

Sift together flour, soda, and salt; set aside. Beat together butter or shortening and brown sugar until fluffy. Add vanilla and egg, beating well. Gradually add dry ingredients and mix thoroughly. Stir in chocolate chips and potato chips. Drop by teaspoonfuls onto ungreased cookie sheets, about 2 inches apart. Bake for 10 to 12 minutes, until lightly browned. Cool on racks. Makes about 5 dozen cookies.

SWEET AND WHOLE-WHEAT COOKIES

Janet Kelman   Royal Oak, Michigan

2 cups whole-wheat flour
¼ cup plain wheat germ
¼ cup nonfat dry milk
1 teaspoon salt (omit if salted butter was used)
1 teaspoon baking soda
½ cup butter, preferably unsalted
½ cup shortening
1 cup brown sugar
⅓ cup molasses
2 eggs
1 teaspoon vanilla
1 package (12 ounces) chocolate chips

Preheat oven to 375° F.

Mix together flour, wheat germ, dry milk, salt, and baking soda; set aside. Beat together butter, shortening, sugar, and molasses. Beat in eggs and vanilla. In two parts, add dry ingredients, beating well. Stir in chocolate chips. Drop by teaspoonfuls onto greased cookie sheets, about 2 inches apart. Bake for 10 to 11 minutes. When the cookies puff up, collapse, and just begin to turn brown, they are done. The cookies will be soft, so remove them carefully from the cookie sheets to racks to cool. Makes about 80 cookies.

MAE'S COWBOY COOKIES

Mae Jones   Rochester, New York

2 cups sifted all-purpose flour
1 teaspoon baking soda
1 teaspoon salt
½ cup wheat germ
1 cup shortening
1 cup brown sugar
1 cup granulated sugar
2 eggs
½ cup plain yogurt
1½ teaspoons vanilla
2 cups rolled oats
1 package (12 ounces) chocolate chips

Preheat oven to 375° F.

Sift together flour, baking soda, and salt; stir in wheat germ and set aside. Beat together shortening and sugars. Add eggs, yogurt, and vanilla and beat by hand 1 minute. Add dry ingredients, then stir in oats and chocolate chips; mix well. Drop by rounded teaspoonfuls onto greased cookie sheets, about 2 inches apart. Bake for 8 to 12 minutes, depending on whether you like them soft and chewy or brown and crunchy. Cool slightly on sheets before removing to racks to cool. Makes about 6 dozen cookies.

CHOCOLATE CHIP OATMEAL DATE COOKIES

Mrs. Donald Toppen   Muskegon, Michigan

3 cups sifted all-purpose flour
1 teaspoon ground cinnamon
1 teaspoon salt
1 teaspoon baking soda
¾ cup margarine
¾ cup lard
1 cup granulated sugar
1 cup brown sugar
3 eggs
1 teaspoon vanilla
3 cups quick oatmeal
½ cup chopped nuts
1 package (6 ounces) chocolate chips
1 cup chopped dates

Preheat oven to 375° F.

Sift together flour, cinnamon, salt, and baking soda; set aside. Beat together margarine, lard, sugars, eggs, and vanilla. Add dry ingredients and oatmeal to creamed mixture. Mix together well. Add nuts, chocolate chips, and dates and mix well. Shape dough into three bars and wrap in waxed paper. Place bars in refrigerator or freezer overnight.

Using a very sharp knife, slice bars into cookies ⅛ inch thick. Bake, as needed, on greased cookie sheet for 12 minutes. Cool on racks. Makes 8 dozen.

COCO-PECAN CHIPS

Mrs. Jack Buckel   Fort Wayne, Indiana

2¼ cups sifted all-purpose flour
1 teaspoon salt
1 teaspoon baking soda
1 cup margarine, softened
1 cup brown sugar
⅔ cup granulated sugar
2 eggs
1 teaspoon vanilla
1 package (12 ounces) chocolate chips
1 cup chopped pecans
½ cup shredded coconut

Preheat oven to 375° F.

Sift together flour, salt, and baking soda; set aside. Beat together margarine, sugars, eggs, and vanilla on low speed for 3 minutes. Add dry ingredients and mix well. Stir in chocolate chips, nuts, and coconut. Drop by rounded teaspoonfuls onto greased cookie sheets about 2 inches apart. Bake for 12 minutes. Cool on brown paper or paper toweling. Makes about 4 dozen cookies.

CHUNKY CHIPPERS

Karen E. Giard   Colrain, Massachusetts

2 cups unsifted all-purpose flour
1 teaspoon baking soda
½ teaspoon salt
½ cup shortening
½ cup chunky peanut butter
2 eggs
1 cup granulated sugar
½ cup brown sugar
1 teaspoon vanilla
1 tablespoon water
1 package (12 ounces) chocolate chips

Preheat oven to 350° F.

Stir together flour, baking soda, and salt; set aside. Beat shortening, peanut butter, eggs, sugars, vanilla, and water until creamy. Add dry ingredients and blend well. Stir in chocolate chips. Drop by teaspoonfuls onto lightly greased baking sheets, about 2 inches apart. Bake for 10 to 12 minutes. Cool on racks. Makes about 70 cookies.

Down at Neiman-Marcus, the extravagant Texas department store, you can get a Monopoly game made completely out of chocolate: dark chocolate for the game board, light milk chocolate for the property deeds, wintergreen for the houses, and cinnamon chocolate for the hotels. It gives a whole new dimension to landing on Boardwalk and Park Place.

CHOCOLATE JEWEL DROPS

Mrs. W. G. Davies   Kirkland, Washington

2¼ cups sifted all-purpose flour
1 teaspoon baking powder
½ teaspoon baking soda
½ teaspoon salt
¾ cup shortening
1 cup granulated sugar
2 eggs
2 tablespoons milk
1 teaspoon vanilla
1 cup chopped nuts
1 cup chopped dates

⅓ cup maraschino cherries, drained and chopped,
  plus about 15 maraschino cherries, cut into
  quarters, for decoration
½ cup shredded coconut
1 package (6 ounces) chocolate chips
2½ cups cornflakes, crushed

Preheat oven to 375° F.

Sift together flour, baking powder, baking soda, and salt; set aside. Beat together shortening and sugar. Add eggs, milk, and vanilla and beat well. Blend in dry ingredients gradually. Mix thoroughly. Add nuts, dates, and chopped maraschino cherries and mix well. Stir in chocolate chips and coconut. Drop by rounded teaspoonfuls into the crushed cornflakes. Toss lightly to coat dough and form into balls. Place on greased cookie sheets, about 1½ inches apart, and top each cookie with a maraschino cherry quarter. Bake for 12 to 15 minutes. Cool on racks. Makes about 5 dozen cookies.

The American Entrepreneurs Association, *a business research and development organization based in Los Angeles, publishes an instruction manual telling how to set up and operate your own chocolate chip cookie shop.*

CHOCO-PUMPKIN CHIPS

Susan L. Warfield   Harrisburg, Pennsylvania

6 cups all-purpose flour
1 teaspoon baking soda
2 teaspoons baking powder
1 teaspoon salt
1⅓ cups shortening
2¼ cups granulated sugar
3 eggs
2 teaspoons vanilla
1 cup cooked fresh pumpkin
1 package (12 ounces) semisweet chocolate chips
1 cup chopped nuts

Preheat oven to 375° F.

Sift together flour, baking soda, baking powder, and salt; set aside. Beat together shortening and sugar. Beat in eggs and vanilla until well blended. Add pumpkin and mix well. Add dry ingredients and blend well. Stir in chocolate chips and nuts. Drop by heaping tablespoonfuls onto greased cookie sheets about 2 inches apart, and flatten slightly. Bake for 10 to 12 minutes; do not brown. Cool on racks. Makes about 4 dozen 4-inch cookies.

CHOCO-GRAPE NUT CRUNCHIES

Carol Ann Zychinski   St. Louis, Missouri

4½ cups sifted all-purpose flour
2 teaspoons baking soda
2 teaspoons salt
1 cup margarine
1 cup shortening
1½ cups brown sugar, firmly packed
1½ cups granulated sugar
4 eggs
2 teaspoons vanilla
1 teaspoon water
1 package (12 ounces) chocolate chips
2 cups Grape Nuts cereal

Preheat oven to 375° F.

Sift together flour, baking soda, and salt; set aside. Beat together shortening, margarine, and sugars until creamy. Beat in eggs. Beat in vanilla and water. Add dry ingredients, a little at a time. Stir in chocolate chips and Grape Nuts. Drop by teaspoonfuls onto greased cookie sheets, about 2 inches apart. Bake for 8 to 10 minutes. Cool on racks. Makes 200 two-inch cookies.

The Nestlé Company, which introduced chocolate chips back in 1939, now produces about 250 million of them each day.

Among the countries of the world, the United States is in seventh place in the amount of chocolate eaten per person each year. On the average, each American eats 10 pounds annually. By comparison, Switzerland is first with 22 pounds per capita followed by England (15.4 pounds), West Germany (13.8 pounds), Belgium (13.6 pounds), and Sweden and Austria tied at 11.6 pounds each.

PEANUT BUTTER SQUARES

Mrs. Hardin Dockins   Sandpoint, Idaho

1 cup unsifted all-purpose flour
1 teaspoon baking powder
¼ teaspoon salt
½ cup peanut butter
⅓ cup butter or margarine, softened
½ cup granulated sugar
½ cup brown sugar, firmly packed
2 eggs
1 teaspoon vanilla
1 package (6 ounces) semisweet chocolate chips

Preheat oven to 350° F.

Mix together flour, baking powder, and salt; set aside. Beat together peanut butter and butter with sugars until fluffy. Beat in eggs and vanilla until blended; stir in dry ingredients until blended. Mix in chocolate chips. Spread in greased 8×8×2-inch pan. Bake for 30 to 35 minutes; do not overbake. Cool in pan and cut into squares. Makes about 16 two-inch-square cookies.

> Montezuma, the emperor of the Aztec Indians in Mexico, was the first known chocoholic. Each day he would drink fifty cups of chocolate while serving another two thousand cups to his royal household.

CHOCOLATE CHIP MELT-A-WAYS

Elizabeth Vanyo Cleveland, Ohio

1 cup plus 2 tablespoons all-purpose flour
½ teaspoon baking soda
½ cup butter
6 tablespoons granulated sugar
6 tablespoons confectioners sugar, sifted
1 egg
½ teaspoon vanilla
1 package (6 ounces) chocolate chips

Preheat oven to 350° F.

Sift together flour and baking soda; set aside. Beat together butter and sugars. Beat in egg and vanilla. Add dry ingredients. Stir in chocolate chips. Drop by teaspoonfuls onto ungreased cookie sheets, about 2 inches apart. Bake for 13 minutes, or until light brown. Cool on racks. Makes about 50 cookies.

Bloomingdale's, the chic and trendy department store, was sued for $7,000,000 by Marion Swaybill, an associate news producer at NBC, who said the store was selling a chocolate chip cookie made from her recipe without paying royalties.

The store admitted that, yes, they were selling a chocolate chip cookie called Bloomingdale's Good Cookie but, no, it was not made from Ms. Swaybill's recipe.

The dispute was finally settled out of court and one can easily picture the plaintiff, the defendant, and the lawyers all sitting around a polished teakwood conference table resolving their differences over chocolate chip cookies and milk.

MALTED CHIP COOKIES

Jeanette Smithson   Costa Mesa, California

1¼ cups unsifted all-purpose flour
¼ cup unsweetened cocoa powder
¼ cup malt powder
½ teaspoon baking soda
½ teaspoon salt
⅓ cup butter, softened
⅓ cup shortening
½ cup granulated sugar
⅓ cup brown sugar
1 tablespoon molasses
1 egg
2 teaspoons vanilla
1 package (6 ounces) unsweetened chocolate chips

Preheat oven to 350° F.

Sift or stir together flour, cocoa powder, malt, baking soda and salt; set aside. Beat together butter, shortening, sugars, and molasses. Beat in egg and vanilla until light and creamy. Blend in dry ingredients. Stir in chocolate chips. Drop by teaspoonfuls onto lightly greased cookie sheet, about 2 inches apart. Bake for 10 to 12 minutes. Cool on racks. Makes about 50 cookies.

PINEAPPLE-OATMEAL CRUNCHIES

Kathy Frisbie   Costa Mesa, California

2 cups sifted all-purpose flour
1 teaspoon baking soda
½ teaspoon salt
1 cup shortening
1 cup granulated sugar
2 eggs
1 can (8¼ ounces) crushed pineapple with juice
1 tablespoon vanilla
2 cups quick oatmeal
1 cup chopped nuts
½ cup shredded coconut
1 package (12 ounces) chocolate chips

Preheat oven to 375° F.

Sift together flour, baking soda, and salt; set aside. Beat together shortening and sugar. Beat in eggs until fluffy. Stir in pineapple, vanilla, and dry ingredients. Blend well. Stir in oatmeal, nuts, coconut, and chocolate chips. Drop by teaspoonfuls onto ungreased cookie sheets, about 2 inches apart. Bake for 12 to 15 minutes. Cool on racks. Makes about 6 dozen cookies.

In a daring and clever action, the Canadian government helped six American diplomats escape from Iran while 50 others were being held hostage in the American Embassy in Teheran.

The response in the United States to this dramatic episode was a tremendous outpouring of praise and gratitude for the Canadians, including telephone calls, telegrams, flowers, cakes in the shape of maple leaves, champagne, and invitations for lunches and dinners.

Along with everything else, the Canadian Consulate General in New York received a two-pound bag of chocolate chip cookies with a note signed "Two Americans" who wrote: "Canadians are chocolate chip all the way."

HONEY CHIPS

Mrs. Louis Smith   Fort Lauderdale, Florida

2¾ cups cake flour
1 teaspoon baking soda
¾ teaspoon salt
1 cup butter or margarine
¾ cup granulated sugar
¾ cup brown sugar
1 teaspoon vanilla
2 eggs
1 teaspoon honey
1 package (12 ounces) chocolate chips
1 cup chopped nuts

Preheat oven to 375° F.
Sift together flour, baking soda, and salt. Beat together butter and sugars. Beat in vanilla until creamy. Beat in eggs, one at a time, then honey. Blend well. Add dry ingredients; mix well. Stir in chocolate chips and nuts. Drop by teaspoonfuls onto greased cookie sheet, about 2 inches apart. Bake about 10 minutes. Cool on racks. Makes about 100 cookies.

CHOCOLATE CHIP PIZZA

Karen Midgarden   Hoople, North Dakota

1 cup sifted all-purpose flour
½ teaspoon baking powder
⅛ teaspoon baking soda
½ teaspoon salt
⅓ cup butter or margarine, melted
1 cup brown sugar, firmly packed
1 egg
1 tablespoon hot water
1¼ teaspoons vanilla
½ cup chopped nuts
1 package (6 ounces) semisweet chocolate chips
1 cup miniature marshmallows

Preheat oven to 350° F.

Sift together flour, baking powder, baking soda, and salt; set aside. With electric mixer, beat melted butter and brown sugar on medium speed till blended. Beat in egg, hot water, and vanilla. Add dry ingredients, one third at a time, mixing well each time. Stir in nuts. Spread dough in two greased 9-inch pie plates. Sprinkle each pie with half the chocolate chips and half the marshmallows. Bake for 20 minutes. Cool in pans on rack. Cut each pie into 8 pieces. Serves 16.

CHOCOLATE SOFTIES

Paula Pace   Bonne Terre, Missouri

1½ cups sifted all-purpose flour
½ cup cornmeal
1 teaspoon baking powder
¼ teaspoon salt
¾ cup shortening
¾ cup granulated sugar
1 egg
1 teaspoon vanilla
½ cup chocolate chips

Preheat oven to 350° F.

Sift together flour, cornmeal, baking powder, and salt; set aside. Beat together shortening and sugar. Add egg and vanilla and beat well. Add dry ingredients. Stir in chocolate chips. Drop by teaspoonfuls onto greased cookie sheet. Bake for about 15 minutes, until lightly browned. Cool on racks. Makes about 3 dozen cookies.

King Louis XIV of France established the position of Royal Chocolate Maker to the King.

CHOCOLATE CHIP ANGEL COOKIES

Mrs. Wayne Roberts   New Ulm, Minnesota

2 cups sifted all-purpose flour
1 teaspoon baking soda
1 teaspoon cream of tartar
¼ teaspoon salt
½ cup butter
½ cup shortening
½ cup brown sugar
½ cup granulated sugar
1 egg
1 teaspoon vanilla
¾ cup broken nuts
1 package (6 ounces) chocolate chips

Preheat oven to 350° F.

Sift together flour, baking soda, cream of tartar, and salt; set aside. Beat together shortening, butter, and sugars. Beat in egg and vanilla. Add sifted dry ingredients. Fold in nuts and chocolate chips. Roll into balls the size of a walnut; roll in sugar. Place on greased cookie sheets. Bake 10 to 12 minutes. Cool on racks. Makes about 60 cookies.

MACADAMIA CREMES

Douglas P. Foglietta   Glenwood, Illinois

1 cup butter
¾ cup brown sugar
¾ cup granulated sugar
2 eggs, beaten
1 teaspoon baking soda
1 teaspoon hot water
2¼ cups sifted all-purpose flour
1 teaspoon salt
1 teaspoon or more creme de cacao (dark)
1 cup chopped macadamia nuts
  (or your choice)
1 package (6 ounces) chocolate chips

Preheat oven to 375° F.

Beat together butter and sugars. Add the beaten eggs and the rest of the ingredients in order listed; fold in the nuts and chocolate chips last. Drop by teaspoonfuls onto greased cookie sheets and bake for 10 to 12 minutes. Makes about 90 cookies.

CHOCOLATE YOGURT MELTS

Debbie Takacs   Fresno, California

1 package devil's food chocolate cake mix
1 carton (8 ounces) cherry yogurt
1 egg, lightly beaten
2 tablespoons margarine, melted
⅔ cup chopped nuts
1 package (6 ounces) chocolate chips

Preheat oven to 350° F.

Stir together cake mix, yogurt, egg, and margarine until thoroughly mixed. Fold in nuts and chocolate chips. Drop by teaspoonfuls onto ungreased cookie sheets. Bake for 12 to 15 minutes. Makes about 90 cookies.

In 1785, Thomas Jefferson sent a letter to John Adams in which he wrote that "The superiority of chocolate drink, both for health and nourishment, will soon give it the same preference over tea and coffee in America which it has in Spain."

The names of the new cookie emporiums clearly advertise their wares: *That Cookie Place* in Los Angeles, *Otis Spunkmeyer Old Tyme Cookie* in San Francisco, the *Chipyard* in Boston, *The Cookie Works, We Got Your Cookie,* and the *Cookie Coach Co.* in New York. And many shopping centers have chain establishments like *The Cookie Machine,* the *Famous Chocolate Chip Cookie, The Cookie Muncher, The Cookie Caper, The Cookie Factory, The Cookie of the Month,* and *The Original Cookie Company.*

The prize for the most bombastic name of all has to go to a store in Manhattan with the ultimate claim: *Absolutely The Best Chocolate Chip Cookie in New York City.*

CINNAMON MARMALADE MORSELS

Susan Hardison   Franklin, Maine

2 cups sifted all-purpose flour
1 teaspoon baking soda
1 teaspoon cinnamon
1 teaspoon nutmeg
½ teaspoon salt
½ cup shortening
1 cup orange marmalade
1 egg
1 teaspoon vanilla
1 package (6 ounces) chocolate chips
1 cup chopped walnuts

Preheat oven to 350° F.

Sift together flour, baking soda, cinnamon, nutmeg, and salt; set aside. Beat together shortening and marmalade. Beat in egg and vanilla. Add sifted dry ingredients. Stir in chocolate chips and walnuts. Drop by teaspoonfuls onto greased cookie sheets, about 2 inches apart. Bake for 10 to 15 minutes. Cool on racks. Makes about 70 cookies.

MELT-IN-THE-MOUTH SQUARES

Joy M. Hall   Lucedale, Mississippi

½ cup butter or margarine (melted)
1 cup graham cracker crumbs
1 cup shredded coconut
1 package (6 ounces) chocolate chips
1 package (6 ounces) butterscotch chips
1 can (13 ounces) sweetened condensed milk
1 cup chopped pecans

Preheat oven to 325° F.

Grease a 9 × 13-inch pan. Make layers using the seven ingredients listed above in the order given. Bake for 25 minutes. Let cool and then cut into blocks. Makes about 30 two-inch square cookies.

When the British imposed a tax on tea many American colonists switched to hot chocolate as their household drink.

Baker's Chocolate claims the oldest grocery trademark in the United States, a painting called "The Beautiful Chocolate Girl."

The girl in the painting is Anna Baltrauf, who was working in a chocolate shop in Vienna back in 1745 when she met Prince Ditrichstein, an Austrian nobleman. They fell in love, got married, and the new bride had her portrait painted, not in the usual formal gown, but in a seventeenth-century dress serving chocolate.

The painting found its way to the Dresden Art Gallery in Germany, where it was seen in 1862 by the president of Baker's Chocolate. He liked "The Beautiful Chocolate Girl" so much that he adopted her as the symbol of his company.

KRISPY DELIGHTS

Merna M. Moulton   Attica, Kansas

1½ cups unsifted all-purpose flour
1 teaspoon salt
1 teaspoon baking soda
1 cup chunky peanut butter
½ cup margarine
1½ cups brown sugar
1 cup granulated sugar
4 eggs, well beaten
2 teaspoons vanilla
3 cups quick oatmeal
1 package (12 ounces) chocolate chips

Preheat oven to 375° F.

Stir together flour, salt, and baking soda; set aside. Beat together peanut butter, margarine, and sugars. Add eggs and vanilla and beat well. Add dry ingredients. Mix well. Stir in oatmeal and chocolate chips. Shape into rolls and refrigerate overnight.

Slice ¼ inch thick. Bake on ungreased cookie sheet 10 minutes, or until browned. Makes 6 dozen cookies.

ALMOND CHIP DROPS

Ruth Roberts   La Place, Louisiana

¾ cup butter
½ cup granulated sugar
1 egg
½ teaspoon vanilla
½ teaspoon almond extract
1 cup chopped almonds
2 cups sifted all-purpose flour
1 package (6 ounces) semisweet chocolate chips

Preheat oven to 375° F.

Beat together butter with sugar until light. Add egg, beating well. Add vanilla and almond extract with flour, mixing until well blended. Lightly stir in almonds and chocolate chips. Drop by teaspoonfuls onto cookie sheet, about 1 inch apart. Bake for 8 to 10 minutes, until a delicate brown. Makes 4½ dozen cookies.

According to Professor Joan Gussow of Columbia University, as quoted in Snack Food magazine, chocolate chip cookies are so admired and desired because: "This country is going through an enormous emotional trauma, and people don't know what to believe. Therefore, we're very susceptible to things we can trust—like a little chocolate chip cookie we can actually see coming out of the oven."

It is impossible to say exactly how many chocolate chip cookies are eaten every year because no one knows. But according to Nabisco, one of the major cookie baking companies in the United States, more than 200 million pounds of packaged chocolate chip cookies are sold annually.

This is an amount equal in weight to nearly 3 battleships, more than 500 fully loaded Boeing 747 jetliners, close to 100,000 automobiles, or about 15,000 hippopotamuses.

GAWLEE! TEENY BOPPERS MINT-CHOCOLATE CHIP COOKIES

Hugh Poole   Conyers, Georgia

COOKIES

1 cup plus 2 tablespoons unsifted all-purpose flour
½ teaspoon baking soda
½ teaspoon salt
½ cup butter or margarine
½ cup granulated sugar
½ cup dark brown sugar
¾ teaspoon peppermint flavoring
1 egg
1 package (6 ounces) semisweet chocolate chips
½ cup chopped walnuts

MINT FROSTING

3 tablespoons butter or margarine, softened
1½ cups confectioner's sugar
Few drops green food coloring
2 tablespoons heavy cream
¾ teaspoon peppermint flavoring

GLAZE TOPPING

1 package (6 ounces) semisweet chocolate chips
4 tablespoons butter or margarine

Preheat oven to 375° F.

Mix together flour, baking soda, and salt; set aside. Beat butter and gradually add the two sugars. Beat until light and smooth. Beat in the flavoring and egg. Add dry ingredients, blending well. Stir in chocolate chips and walnuts. Drop by teaspoonfuls onto greased cookie sheets, about 1 inch apart. Bake for 8 to 10 minutes, or until lightly browned. Cool on racks.

Combine all ingredients for MINT FROSTING and blend until creamy. Spread on cooled cookies. Refrigerate while making GLAZE TOPPING.

Combine all glaze topping ingredients and melt in top of double boiler over simmering water. Blend well. Spread glaze over mint-frosted cookies. Refrigerate. Makes about 4 dozen cookies.

It is estimated by food industry officials that one half of all cookies baked at home are chocolate chip cookies.

Captain Cookie, a creative bakery delivery service, will deliver a 15-pound, 2½ foot-in-diameter chocolate chip cookie anywhere in the New York City area for $150.

The Chipwich is an ice cream sandwich made with chocolate chip cookies. It was created by Richard LaMotta, who spent months in a test kitchen he had set up in the basement of his father's house in Brooklyn developing a chocolate chip cookie that would not get soggy from the ice cream.

LaMotta has become a millionaire and gained 20 pounds since inventing the Chipwich.

PEANUTTY CHOCOLATE CHIPS

Elaine A. Carsey   Omaha, Nebraska

4½ cups sifted all-purpose flour
2 teaspoons baking soda
2 teaspoons salt
2 cups shortening
1½ cups granulated sugar
1½ cups brown sugar
2 teaspoons vanilla
1 teaspoon water
4 eggs
1 cup chopped peanuts
1 package (12 ounces) chocolate chips

Preheat oven to 375° F.

Sift together flour, baking soda, and salt; set aside. Beat shortening, sugars, vanilla, and water until creamy. Beat in eggs, one at a time. Add dry ingredients and mix well. Stir in peanuts and chocolate chips. Drop by teaspoonfuls onto greased cookie sheets, about 2 inches apart. Bake for 10 to 12 minutes. Makes about 98 cookies.

The 16,000 *annual visitors to Hershey's Chocolate World in Hershey, Pennsylvania, learn that Hershey is the largest single user of almonds in the United States (all of them grown in California) and that the company did no advertising during the first sixty-eight years it was in business. And the chocolate kisses, first made in 1907, are produced at the rate of 20 million a day.*

MOCHA FROSTED DROPS

Opal N. Kingsbury   Windsor, Wisconsin

COOKIES

½ cup butter
2 ounces (2 squares) unsweetened chocolate
1 cup brown sugar, firmly packed
1 egg
½ teaspoon vanilla
½ cup buttermilk
1½ cups sifted all-purpose flour
½ teaspoon baking soda

½ teaspoon baking powder
¼ teaspoon salt
½ cup chopped walnuts
1 package (6 ounces) chocolate chips, preferably mint flavored

MOCHA FROSTING

4 tablespoons butter
2 tablespoons unsweetened cocoa powder
2 teaspoons instant coffee powder
Dash of salt
2½ cups sifted confectioner's sugar
1½ teaspoons vanilla
Milk
50 walnut halves, or as needed

Preheat oven to 375° F.

Melt butter and chocolate together in saucepan. Cool 10 minutes. Stir in brown sugar. Beat in egg, vanilla, and buttermilk. Sift together dry ingredients and add to egg mixture; mix well. Stir in nuts and chocolate chips. Drop by teaspoonfuls onto greased cookie sheet, about 2 inches apart. Bake for about 10 minutes. Cool on racks.

Meanwhile, make frosting. Beat together butter, cocoa powder, instant coffee powder, and salt. Beat in sugar, vanilla, and enough milk for a spreading consistency. Spread MOCHA FROSTING on cooled cookies and top each with a walnut half. Makes about 50 cookies.

BANANA CHOCOLATE CHIPS

Anne Kissel   Churchville, New York

    3 cups unsifted all-purpose flour
    4½ teaspoons baking powder
    1 teaspoon baking soda
    1½ teaspoons salt
    1 cup butter
    ¾ cup granulated sugar
    ½ cup light brown sugar, firmly packed
    1 egg
    1 teaspoon vanilla or orange extract
    1 cup mashed bananas
    1 package (12 ounces) semisweet chocolate chips
    1 cup chopped pecans or walnuts

Preheat oven to 350° F.

Stir together flour, baking powder, salt, and baking soda; set aside. Beat together butter and sugars. Add egg and vanilla, beating well. Blend in bananas. Add dry ingredients, blending well. Stir in chocolate chips and nuts. Drop by tablespoonfuls onto greased cookie sheets, about 2 inches apart. Bake for 12 to 14 minutes. Cool on racks. Makes about 6 dozen cookies.

ITALIAN CHOCOLATE CHIP COOKIES

Mrs. Pasqualia Oransky   Richboro, Pennsylvania

½ cup granulated sugar
½ cup olive oil or melted butter
½ cup water
1 teaspoon baking powder
½ cup seedless raisins, soaked overnight in 1 cup
    water and 1 tablespoon rum, drained
1 package (6 ounces) semisweet chocolate chips
¼ cup pine nuts
¼ teaspoon salt
4 cups all-purpose flour
Confectioners sugar (optional)

Preheat oven to 375° F.

Mix together sugar, oil, water, baking powder, drained raisins, chocolate chips, pine nuts, and salt. Add flour and mix well. Drop by 2-teaspoonfuls onto ungreased cookie sheets, about 2 inches apart. Bake for 12 minutes. Cool on racks and sprinkle with confectioners sugar, if desired. Store in airtight containers to keep well. Makes about 6½ dozen cookies.

CHEWY CHIP BARS

Alice Wallace   Caballo, New Mexico

½ box (9½ ounces) yellow or chocolate cake mix
2 eggs
1 cup brown sugar, firmly packed
2 tablespoons melted butter
2 tablespoons honey
1 cup chocolate chips
1 cup chopped walnuts or pecans

Preheat oven to 350° F.

Combine all ingredients in large bowl until just blended. Spread in a well-greased 9 × 13-inch baking pan. Bake 30 minutes. Cut into bars or squares. Makes about 30 two-inch squares.

Napoleon always carried chocolate with him on military campaigns and would eat it whenever he wanted quick energy.

NOEL CHOCOLATE CHIP COOKIES

Beatriz G. de Ordonez   San Antonio, Texas

2¼ cups sifted all-purpose flour
1 teaspoon baking soda
1 teaspoon salt
1 cup granulated sugar
½ cup brown sugar, firmly packed
2 eggs
1 teaspoon vanilla
1 cup vegetable shortening
1 cup chopped nuts
1½ cups chocolate chips
¾ cup coarsely chopped candied pineapple
¾ cup coarsely chopped red or green (or both)
    candied cherries

Preheat oven to 375° F.

Stir together flour, soda, and salt. Add the sugars, eggs, vanilla, and shortening. Blend thoroughly. Stir in nuts, chips, and candied pineapple and cherries. Drop by teaspoonfuls onto ungreased baking sheets, about 2 inches apart. Bake for 10 to 12 minutes. Cool on racks. Makes about 100 cookies.

GOOD 'N OATS NUGGETS

Chris Harris   Honolulu, Hawaii

1 cup unsifted all-purpose flour
1 teaspoon baking soda
½ teaspoon salt
¾ cup margarine
1⅓ cups brown sugar, firmly packed
2 eggs
1 teaspoon vanilla
2¾ cups quick oats
¼ cup plain wheat germ
1 package (6 ounces) semisweet chocolate chips

Preheat oven to 350° F.

Stir together flour, baking soda, and salt. Beat together margarine and sugar until light and fluffy. Blend in eggs and vanilla. Add dry ingredients and mix well. Stir in oats, wheat germ, and chocolate pieces. Drop by tablespoonfuls onto greased cookie sheets, about 2 inches apart. Bake for 15 to 17 minutes or until lightly browned. Cool on racks. Makes about 2 dozen cookies.

DERBY CITY CHIPS

Lois Magnus   Louisville, Kentucky

    1 cup sifted all-purpose flour
    ½ teaspoon baking soda
    ½ teaspoon salt
    ½ pound sweet baking chocolate
    ½ cup butter or shortening
    ½ cup granulated sugar
    ¼ cup brown sugar, firmly packed
    1 egg, well beaten
    ½ cup chopped pecans
    1 tablespoon vanilla

Preheat oven to 350° F.

Sift together flour, baking soda, and salt; set aside. Cut each small square of chocolate into 6 or 8 pieces; set aside. Beat together butter and sugars. Beat in egg. Add dry ingredients in two parts. Stir in nuts, chocolate, and vanilla. Drop by teaspoonfuls onto greased cookie sheets, about 2 inches apart. Bake for 10 to 12 minutes. Cool on racks. Makes 50 cookies.

INDEX